IN THE HEARTS
OF GIANTS

ISBN: 978-1-5272-2984-6

First published in 2018 by Newhall Publishing

and

Liverpool City Council
Cunard Building,
Water Street,
Liverpool L3 1DS

British Library cataloguing-in-publication information
A British Library CIP record is available for this title

Printed and bound in the UK by Swallowtail Print Ltd

CONTENTS

FOREWORD

T here are many things I'm proud of as Mayor of Liverpool, but seeing first-hand the impact of a major cultural event on people who live, work and visit this great city is truly humbling.

Pre-2008, if anyone had raised the idea of Giants exploring the city's streets, it would probably have been filed under 'nice thought, but not something we can do'.

But things began to change in 2003 when the city was awarded the 2008 European Capital of Culture title. Liverpool got its swagger back.

Physically this city changed – regeneration projects flourished and the cityscape grew before our very eyes. And as it grew, so did our confidence.

As Scousers, we have always been proud of the city and never doubted its potential, but now, thanks to a cultural title that came with an international spotlight, we could show the world the real Liverpool. The Liverpool that embraces its diverse communities and celebrates the world in one city. The Liverpool that isn't afraid to push boundaries in the name of entertainment and art. The Liverpool that aspires to be a creative hub. The Liverpool that is open for business. The Liverpool where people want to live, work and play.

This is a city that's a hot bed of cultural activity, and we are quite rightly considered a global exemplar when it comes to staging major events. And they don't get much more major than the Giants.

I first met Jean-Luc back in 2010. He had spent time here researching the history of the city's relationship with the Titanic and had quite quickly fallen in love with Liverpool. I can safely say I have never met a character like him – his passion for the city along with his creative talents left me in no doubt that this is someone who would produce a unique and unforgettable show.

Eight years on, and the Liverpool-Nantes relationship remains strong.

From the outset we knew Liverpool's Dream would be the finale in the Giants trilogy and it would be one last Liverpool goodbye to our Giant friends. However, it came as a surprise to us all to learn that this would be the last ever time these Giants would be seen anywhere in the world.

When the news broke, the outpouring of love for Royal de Luxe from those who had been lucky enough to experience their magic was overwhelming, and not unsurprising. The Little Girl Giant, her playful canine Xolo and the other members of the Giants family had become part of our family, and families across the globe. We had welcomed them into our communities, explored city streets alongside them, cried with them, laughed with them.

Once again the international spotlight was on Liverpool – we were going to be the last-ever city to stage these incredible creations.

The buzz around the event transformed into a loud roar.

But if there was ever a city that could live up to the hype, thrive under the pressure and bask in the attention, it was ours.

And this city shone.

From the moment the sandal appeared in Canning Dock, it was all anyone could talk about. We'd been here before, but it still felt new and exhilarating.

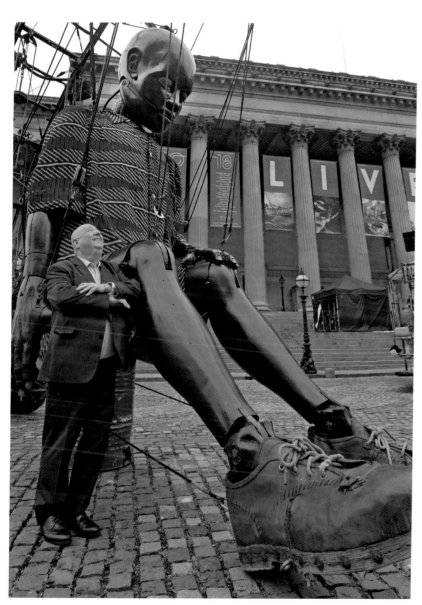

LIVERPOOL ISN'T AFRAID TO PUSH BOUNDARIES IN THE NAME OF ENTERTAINMENT AND ART

Huge crowds were expected and, once again, the public did not disappoint. We didn't think it could get bigger than 2014, but it did and it became the city's biggest ever event to date.

Each day people flocked to see the Little Boy Giant, Xolo and the Giant. Those who have experienced the Royal de Luxe magic before came to see it for one last time, and a whole new audience, some of who weren't even born when they last travelled to our shores, were lucky enough to be part of this moment in history.

The cheers of delight which erupted from the tens of thousands of people on the Waterfront when the Little Girl Giant made a surprise appearance for the finale will stay with me for years to come.

This is art at its best. Creating memories. Bringing together communities. Making us proud that we are a city that can deliver on a Giant scale time and time again.

The end to our Giant Spectacular saga heralds a new, exciting chapter for Royal de Luxe. We wish them well in their new ventures, and I believe I speak on behalf of everyone who has experienced the pleasure their creations generate when I say thank you.

Thank you for your wonderful storytelling.

Thank you for helping meet this city's creative ambitions.

Thank you for three unforgettable events.

Thank you for the Giants.

Joe Anderson

**Joe Anderson OBE,
Mayor of Liverpool**

MY JOURNEY WITH

GIANTS

Liverpool's Director of Culture, Claire McColgan MBE, talks about how the Giants enchanted an entire city.

W ay back in 2006, I took over as Executive Producer for Capital of Culture, and was part of a team that had a passion for supporting and encouraging creativity in our communities.

Showcasing this amazing city to the rest of the world in a way that hadn't been done before was our ambition – whether that was through huge outdoor concerts, intimate projects in parks or epic all-consuming Giant-like endeavours.

In 2006, I sat in Keith's Wine Bar on Lark Lane – with a cup of tea, of course – with Jean-Luc as he drew the Giant in a diver's suit, pitching him as a survivor of the Titanic.

As we got closer to the centenary anniversary in 2012, I knew there was only one company I wanted to work with. Royal de Luxe's style complements the Liverpool character.

There is no other city in the country that has an audience that delights in culture so much. It is

a storytelling city, a city that wears its heart on its sleeve, a port where influences from around the world inform its tolerance and sense of social justice and stimulates debate.

From the moment the Little Girl Giant opened her eyes in 2012 to the moment she left a sunlit waterfront in 2018, the Giants have created a new Liverpool story.

Walking the streets, feeling them fizz with pure joy – adults and children in a world of their own imaginations, in a world beyond the everyday, is an absolute career high for me.

That's why in this city, we believe that culture is essential. Without our orchestras, our galleries, our school plays, or our poetry we are a place of bricks and mortar.

The city belongs to everyone. It is a living, breathing entity made up of the stories it tells.

A weekend of street theatre, aided by road closures and travel timetable changes, enabled Liverpool to bring together more than 1.3 million people. In a time of world uncertainty, where the narrative is around political constructs, Liverpool put its faith in the dreams of Giants, the dreams of people in a story that transcends borders and will live longer than all of us.

I have been so proud to be part of this city's journey. To see what we have achieved has been incredibly rewarding.

But this is just the start of another chapter.

If we look back to 2008, I don't think anyone could have predicted that through austerity, this city would continue to deliver epic ideas on a grand scale and support a thriving year-round culture sector that continuously breaks all visitor records.

This is just the start for Liverpool.

Claire McColgan MBE
Director of Culture for Liverpool

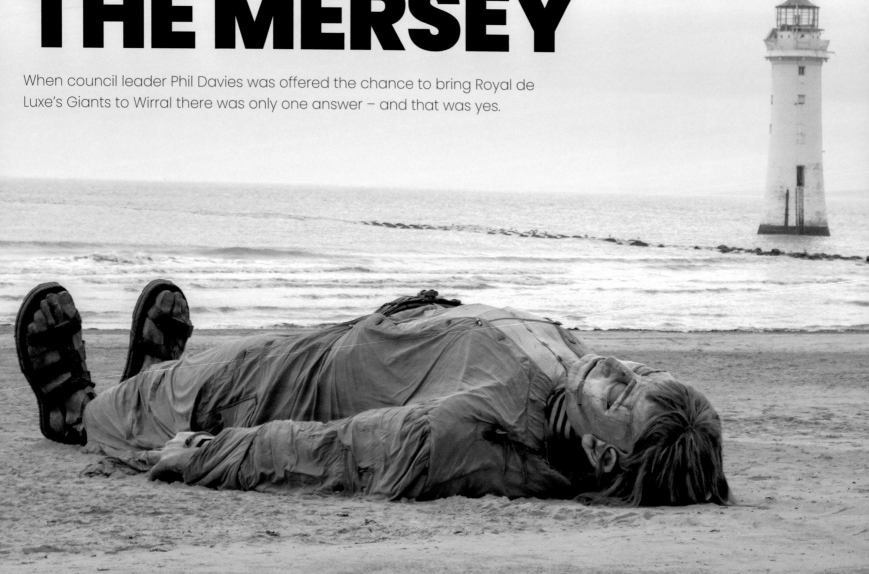

GIANTS ACROSS THE MERSEY

When council leader Phil Davies was offered the chance to bring Royal de Luxe's Giants to Wirral there was only one answer – and that was yes.

Having seen the work of the French street theatre company on its previous visits to Liverpool, Phil Davies knew the opportunity to give the people of Wirral something to remember – and put the peninsula firmly on the national and international map – was too good to miss.

Still, the result was beyond all his expectations, with an estimated 80,000 people flocking to New Brighton to see the Giant roam the waterfront esplanade on the opening day of Liverpool's Dream.

And the excited crowds were captured on camera, beamed in to the nation's front rooms at the start of the evening news and placing Wirral firmly centre stage in the global coverage of this final Giant adventure.

The council leader from West Kirby reveals he "felt quite emotional" throughout the day as the Giant adventure unfolded in front of him.

But it all began with a slightly surreal encounter.

"I did some media interviews first thing on the Friday morning," he recalls. "I was there about 7am, and the Giant sleeping on the shore in front of the iconic New Brighton Lighthouse and Fort Perch Rock with the Liverpool skyline as the backdrop, was just amazing.

"I use the word atmospheric – it was quite eerie, actually, because it was quite overcast, the sea mist was gathering around the beach and there was this 33ft figure sprawled out on the sand.

"There were just a few photographers and cameramen setting up, and one or two dog walkers and kids on bikes, and it was just the most amazing vista when you panned across the beach to see this figure.

"I felt quite emotional throughout the whole day, partly because it was in my backyard, in Wirral, and it was great to have them in the borough, but just being so close to them as well.

"It was just an incredibly strange feeling, a bit of an out-of-body experience, this amazing figure walking around the town."

Cllr Davies was on the balcony of the Floral Pavilion when the Giant rose from the beach at the start of a three-day adventure.

And it was there he experienced one of his own personal highlights of the day. "I had my two grandchildren with me," he explains. "One of them is four months old, so she couldn't really appreciate it, but my grandson is 17 months and he's just started walking and being aware of life around him.

"When he saw the Giant his eyes nearly popped out of his head! It was just incredible. I know it's a bit corny, but this is something that will live in people's memories for years and years. People will say 'I was at New Brighton on the day the

Giant woke up and walked off the beach'. And to see my grandson's reaction was a personal highlight."

He adds: "It definitely surpassed my expectations as an event and as a spectacle, and as a way of enabling us to showcase the wonderful place that we call home, which is the Wirral."

The Giant Spectacular is the latest in a series of cross-river cultural collaborations between Wirral and Liverpool that started with the Three Queens in 2015 and includes the annual River of Light firework extravaganza, Three Festivals Tall Ships Regatta and this summer's Lost Castles.

"People in Merseyside and Liverpool don't differentiate between local authority boundaries on a map," Cllr Davies reasons. "Wirral residents will travel to Liverpool for events, and Liverpool people will come over to Wirral. That's been happening regularly, and this joint working has been promoting that.

"I think it's great that we can market and promote both sides of the river as part of a package that can attract visitors to come to the city region as well as people who already live here."

Liverpool's Dream has also been a major part of Imagine Wirral, launched earlier this year to draw together a series of creative and cultural

events aimed at helping place the borough on an international stage and increasing visitor numbers along with participation in transformative experiences.

And that cultural drive is about to step up a gear, with Wirral being the next community to take on the mantle of Liverpool City Region's Borough of Culture title for 2019.

The title, which rotates between the six boroughs that make up the City Region, comes with a £300,000 commitment for arts and culture from Liverpool Metro Mayor Steve Rotheram's single investment fund.

Wirral is putting the finishing touches to an exciting programme of events themed around the ideas of discovery, exploration and the great outdoors.

With a Giant visit successfully under its belt, and a giant year of culture to come, these are exciting times in Wirral.

Cllr Davies agrees, saying: "We very much see the work we've done as the building blocks for our Borough of Culture year.

"I'm really looking forward to it. I think it's going to be a really exciting year, and I can't wait for it all to be unveiled."

Phil Davies

Cllr Phil Davies
Leader of Wirral Council

INSPIRING THE NEXT GENERATION

Merseyside may have woken from its magical Giant dream – but the legacy of the Giants' visit lives on in the creative minds of thousands of young fans.

The joy of the Giants is that they inhabit a world in which the spectators are more than just passive onlookers.

For the thousands who lined the streets of Liverpool and New Brighton over four fantastic days in October – whether eight months, eight or 80 years old – they were all part of a shared experience.

And none more so than the schoolchildren who had been anticipating this final visit since it was first announced. Some had seen the Giants in 2012 or 2014, but for many this was their first – and only – chance to engage with these Giant characters. And they certainly made the most of it.

As the Little Boy Giant and the Mexican god-dog Xolo made their way along Princes Avenue and into Princes Park on the first day of Liverpool's Dream they were greeted, not just by shouts of excitement and faces full of wonder, but by handmade signs held aloft by the young crowds which read 'Bonjour

Petit Garçon' and 'Salut'. In front of the hundreds of schoolchildren, dozens of richly and creatively-decorated picnic blankets were laid out like welcome banners along the route. 13,000 children from almost 40 schools and community groups from all over the city took part in the mass picnic event.

Meanwhile, across the water in Wirral, children had also been given the day off school to witness the walk of the big Giant – a mysterious figure who had appeared early that morning, washed up on the beach in the shadow of New Brighton's landmark lighthouse.

And they too had come ready for a party, carrying their own bespoke, brightly patterned rugs and blankets which they had carefully crafted in classrooms throughout the borough.

The picnic blankets formed part of a dream-themed participation programme which – as on the previous two visits of Royal de Luxe's amazing creations –

was an integral part of the Giant Spectacular, engaging both young people and communities alike. Ahead of the arrival of the Giants, the city's giants of football took over Princes Park for a series of coaching sessions with a twist. It was a Liverpool city engineer, John Brodie, who invented the first goal net in 1889. Elsewhere, on street corners and in open green spaces, generations of children have been happy to use jumpers as goalposts. But what about a massive piece of footwear?

Liverpool, Everton and Tranmere Rovers ran free football sessions for nine to 11 year olds from 30 primary schools on the day before the Giant picnic in the park. While 11 to 12 year olds from ten secondary schools where given the same opportunity on the morning the Little Boy Giant headed for Toxteth and a well-earned siesta. A Giant's sandal acted as a target for their fast, furious and fun penalty shoot-out.

Along with picnic blankets, there was also a chance for community groups including Granby & Dingle Surestart Children's Centres, Anfield Community Arts, The Greenhouse Project and Adventure Playground (Garston) to make dreamcatchers, inspired by Royal de Luxe's dreamy story.

And Friends of Princes Park produced several huge versions of the woven Native American hoops, made from traditional willow sourced in the park itself and displayed in its Wood Henge.

All this creative inspiration came to a crescendo in two Giant Dreams exhibitions, curated by Vari Kenny and Maria Hann, which ran on either side of the River Mersey throughout the month of October. The curators incorporated artwork created by schools and community groups in to Sinking Sails – an installation in Mann Island made completely from brilliantly-decorated T-shirts, football shirts and pyjama tops, and designed to both reflect Liverpool's maritime heritage and also to ensure everyone's dreams could set sail as the ship floated away.

In fact, so many T-shirts were decorated that there were enough left over to create unique dream-inspired bunting to decorate the waterfront space.

Youngsters also let their imaginations run riot, producing large canvases and crafting their own recyclable Giants from cardboard.

More than 45 Liverpool schools and community organisations were involved in the Sinking Sails project, including Gateacre Comprehensive, Sudley Infants, Little Angels Nursery, Crosby Brownies, Liverpool Children in Council Care and Unity Youth Club.

And hundreds of children from Wirral created artwork for its sister exhibition, Sleeping Whirlwind, which was staged concurrently in the historic surroundings of Birkenhead Priory.

More than 20 schools and community groups reacted to the theme of dreaming, with curators Maria and Vari's installation exploring the components of dreams and how these are formed during our resting moments, with the Sleeping Whirlwind of the title acting as a tornado sweeping together those dreams, aspirations and experiences.

THE TEAM BEHIND

THE GIANTS

Royal de Luxe is without doubt an extraordinary street theatre company.

S ince its creation in 1979, Royal de Luxe has travelled around the world with its small and large scale shows – with creator and Artistic Director, the enigmatic Jean-Luc Courcoult at the helm. The Nantes-based company is invited into the heart of the cities and towns, and is encouraged to devise a show which will surprise and entertain people, regardless of their age, giving them the opportunity to escape from reality for a short time.

Settled in Nantes at the invitation of the Mayor of the City in 1989, Royal de Luxe is nowadays considered as emblematic of street theatre and as a jewel of the French cultural fame over the world. Wherever this unique troop plays it brings enthusiasm, media interest and economic success. In recognition of this, Jean-Luc Courcoult was decorated with the title of Knight of the Order of the Arts and Letters of the French Republic by Jean-Marc Ayrault, Prime Minister of France.

It was in 1993 that Royal de Luxe's work began to cause ripples across the globe. The company unveiled the first of the Giant family and took street theatre to a whole new, Giant level. Royal de Luxe soon became synonymous with ambitious, extravagant theatre – and the saga of the Giants began and became part of the company's history, bringing them to emblematic cities all around the world such as Perth, London, Montreal, Santiago, Reykjavík and Berlin.

Manipulated by dutiful Lilliputians, these Giants transcended fantasy and became part of people's reality. Audiences were engrossed by the poetry unfolding before them, mixing time and genres, with different characters moving at the same time at various ends of a city.

The Giants are widely loved – each year thousands of letters, emails, photos, drawings, true declarations of friendship and love are sent to the company from all over the world.

The company has performed in front of more than 26 million spectators, with around 1,500 shows in 173 cities in 40 countries over five continents.

Liverpool is honoured to hold a very special place in the creative heart of Royal de Luxe. The relationship between this world famous port city and this globally renowned arts organisation is both respectful and beautiful. Both appreciate the other's dedication to pushing creative boundaries and place real value on the importance of bringing culture to all. The power of art is undeniable and the pride it engenders in a community is priceless.

With these connections, it made sense that the final showcase for these Giants should take place in Liverpool. The city was a home from home, and there was nowhere else they could imagine which would give a fitting and deserving farewell to these much-loved characters. And what a send-off it was. The Giants may have departed to a distant land, but their memories and impact will live on in the hearts and minds of more than a million people who were lucky enough to share the experience. Liverpool thanked Royal de Luxe, and in return Royal de Luxe thanked Liverpool in true Giant style.

Dreams don't sleep.

Like a tree on the moon
the Giant, lying on a raft
has stranded on the beach of New Brighton.

Who knows on what ship he has taken off his diving suit,
what storms he has suffered from
and what currents have pushed him towards Liverpool.

The fact remains that the Little Girl Giant has appointed her
brother, the Little Boy Giant, to go to see him.
He has settled in St George's Hall.

Besides the City has organised a fancy dress ball in his honour.
Even if thunder wanted to crush the city,
sewn clouds are protecting the sky.

The heart of the inhabitants radiates so strongly
that we can hear the beats echoing
over to Dublin.

Careful, the dreams of the Giants alight
in Liverpool!

© Written by Jean-Luc Courcoult,
Author and Artistic Director, Founder of Royal de Luxe.

THURSDAY

4 OCTOBER 2018

Ssshhh... don't wake a sleeping Giant!

There was an undeniable buzz around the city. Signs that our Giant friends were heading to our shores had already begun to appear. A mysterious telegram sent to the city overnight, a Giant sandal caught up in a fishing net, a butter knife had landed and cut through an Arriva bus outside Lime Street Station and the appearance of a strange-looking larger-than-life raft floating in the middle of Canning Dock...

Finally, a first sighting of what everyone had been waiting for – the Little Boy Giant fast asleep inside St George's Hall.

On a crisp, dry autumnal day, more than 15,000 people headed to the Grade I-listed building, many in fancy dress costume and masks, lining the plateau for a sneak peek of the snoozing child who was making his first-ever UK appearance.

Inside the Hall, young and old stood in awe as they took in the sights and loud snoring sounds of the Little Boy Giant. There was a real sense that the adventure was about to begin.

And as the night drew in, the party atmosphere escalated, buoyed along by a warm welcome from Royal de Luxe's Artistic Director Jean-Luc Courcoult and some dance-inducing live music.

For one Giant, the temptation to join in the festivities proved too much. Waking up from a secret slumber beside the Hall, mischievous canine Xolo made an unexpected appearance, delighting the crowds as he scampered up William Brown Street and along Lime Street.

And so it began. People had been given a taste of what the next few days had in store and they couldn't wait. It was set to be a breathtaking weekend.

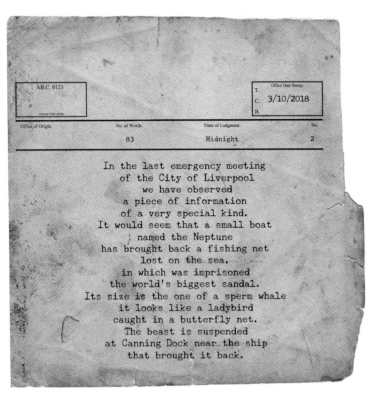

AB.C. 0123

Office Date Stamp.
T.
C. 3/10/2018
B.

(PLEASE TURN OVER)

Office of Origin.	No. of Words.	Time of Lodgment.	No.
	83	Midnight	2

In the last emergency meeting
of the City of Liverpool
we have observed
a piece of information
of a very special kind.
It would seem that a small boat
named the Neptune
has brought back a fishing net
lost on the sea,
in which was imprisoned
the world's biggest sandal.
Its size is the one of a sperm whale
it looks like a ladybird
caught in a butterfly net.
The beast is suspended
at Canning Dock near the ship
that brought it back.

In Liverpool
dreams are strange.

They take you by surprise,
and run through your veins, like night trains,
without station,
slumbering on the infinity of the tracks
destined to lead somewhere.

This neverland.
The last dream of this Giant we left as a
Diver turned him into a shipwrecked
castaway, lost on a raft.

Liverpool is a storm,
one of those that tears off the sailors' bodies.

Despite his strengh the sea propelled this

Giant far from his raft.

Trampled by the waves,
Tossed into the ocean's torrent
smashing his face against the freighters,
he ended up floating,
far from everything...

He found himself lying on a beach, in New
Brighton:
a survivor, a migrant forced to forge a new
memory for himself.

Some Liverpudlians found his raft very far away
in the Arctic.

And brought it back to Canning Dock
So that he could leave at last...

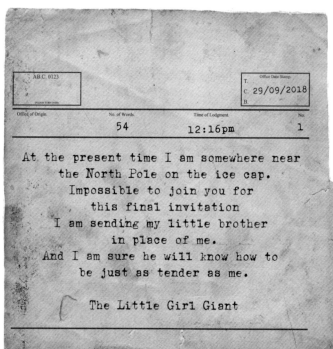

AB.C. 0123

Office Date Stamp.

T.
C. 29/09/2018
B.

(PLEASE TURN OVER)

Office of Origin.	No. of Words.	Time of Lodgment.	No.
	54	12:16pm	1

At the present time I am somewhere near
the North Pole on the ice cap.
Impossible to join you for
this final invitation
I am sending my little brother
in place of me.
And I am sure he will know how to
be just as tender as me.

The Little Girl Giant

EXIT

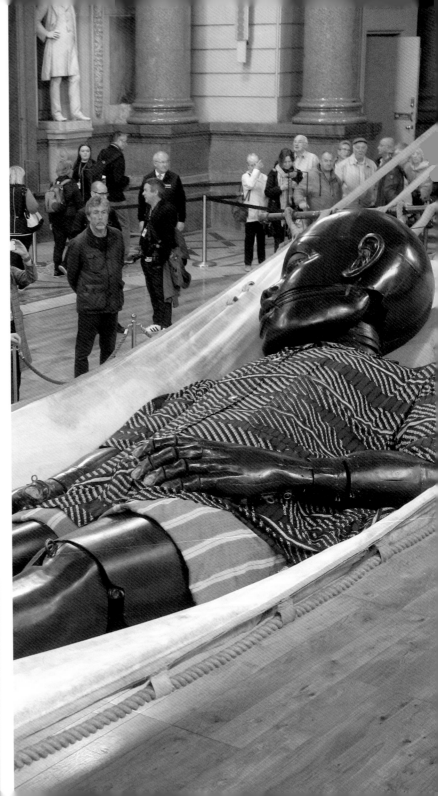

FRIDAY

5 OCTOBER 2018

The Giant adventure gets underway.

The day had arrived that had been nearly two years in the planning. Over in Wirral, a lone Giant figure had washed up on the beach next to the lighthouse at Fort Perch Rock. As the sun rose, curious onlookers gathered on the sand in anticipation of him waking from his slumber – the crowd reacted with gasps and cheers as his eyes slowly opened and he sat up. He was serenaded by a lone violin player sat atop a truck filled with hundreds of violins, playing 'The Leaving of Liverpool'. It was time to explore New Brighton.

He headed on to Marine Promenade, watched by tens of thousands of people. Feeling thirsty as he got to the halfway point of his stroll, Mersey Fire and Rescue Service obliged by spraying gallons of water into his mouth through a huge funnel from a platform 30 feet high. After a siesta at the Dips, he made a return journey, had another drink by the Floral Pavilion before leaving for Liverpool with applause from the crowds ringing in his ears. He later slumbered on his raft for a restful night's sleep.

Over in Liverpool, thousands gathered around St George's Hall to see the Little Boy Giant and Xolo wake up and take in their surroundings. Xolo was the first to open his eyes, an affectionate lick to the boy's hand brought him out of his slumber and he was ready for action! Scampering ahead, Xolo took charge, sniffing and drooling on crowds, and even taking some time out to receive a manicure from a local beauty salon. The Little Boy Giant took in the scenes and the crowds, at one point hitching a ride in a car as his legs grew tired.

The pair made their way towards Princes Park where they were welcomed by hundreds of schoolchildren holding handmade blankets aloft featuring designs of their own Liverpool Dreams.

After a spot of lunch – a bowl of scouse (naturally) – they were ready for a nap ahead of an afternoon exploring again.

Following their snooze, Xolo and the Little Boy Giant were raring to go and headed back into the city centre. Huge numbers of people lined the route, eager to catch a glimpse of them. Queens Wharf provided an uplifting end to the day as Xolo fell asleep in a bed 30 feet up in the air while the Little Boy Giant fell asleep in his flying car!

And as the show came to an end, there were not just two Giants in Liverpool, but three – asleep on a raft in the middle of Canning Dock was the Giant.

NEW BRIGHTON

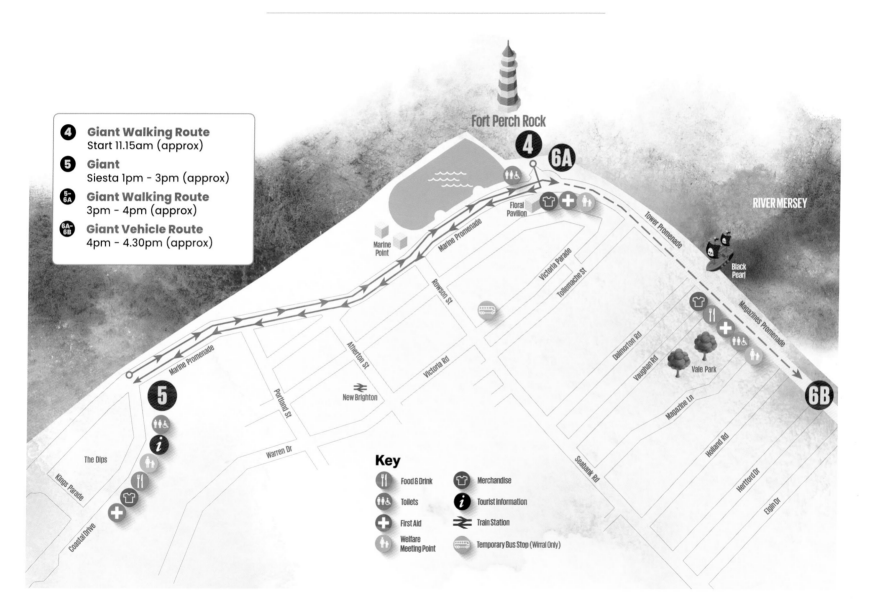

4 Giant Walking Route
Start 11.15am (approx)

5 Giant
Siesta 1pm - 3pm (approx)

5-6A Giant Walking Route
3pm - 4pm (approx)

6A-6B Giant Vehicle Route
4pm - 4.30pm (approx)

Fort Perch Rock

RIVER MERSEY

Floral Pavilion

Marine Point

Marine Promenade

Tower Promenade

Black Pearl

Magazines Promenade

Rowson St

Victoria Parade

Tollemache St

Calmorton Rd

Vaughan Rd

Vale Park

Atherton St

Victoria Rd

New Brighton

Magazine Ln

Portland St

Seabank Rd

Holland Rd

Hertford Dr

Warren Dr

Elgin Dr

The Dips

Kings Parade

Coastal Drive

Key

Food & Drink	Merchandise
Toilets	Tourist Information
First Aid	Train Station
Welfare Meeting Point	Temporary Bus Stop (Wirral Only)

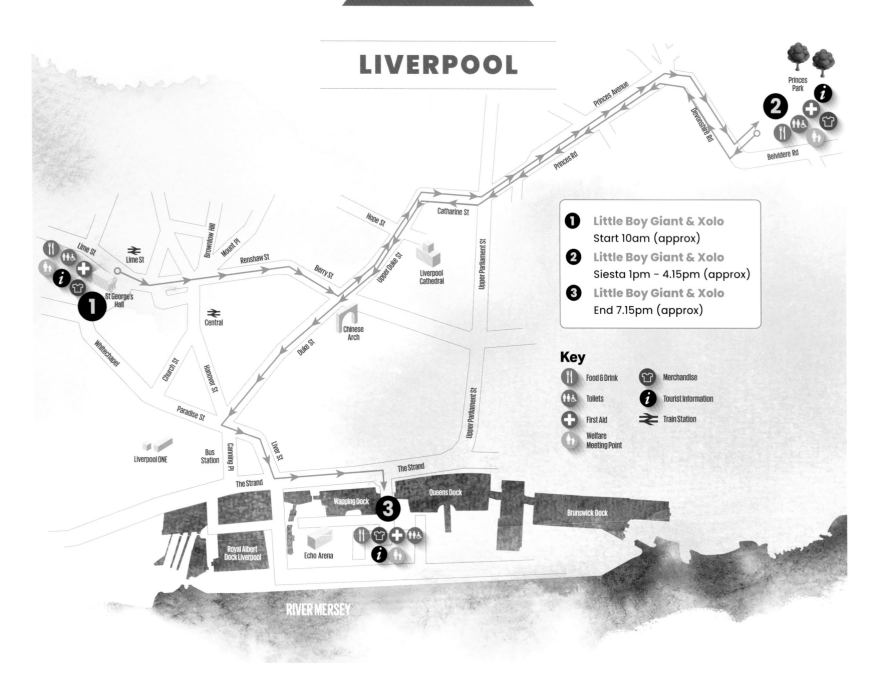

LIVERPOOL

1 **Little Boy Giant & Xolo**
Start 10am (approx)

2 **Little Boy Giant & Xolo**
Siesta 1pm – 4.15pm (approx)

3 **Little Boy Giant & Xolo**
End 7.15pm (approx)

Key

🍴 Food & Drink

🚻 Toilets

➕ First Aid

👪 Welfare Meeting Point

👕 Merchandise

𝒊 Tourist Information

🚉 Train Station

Princes Park

Lime St

Brownlow Hill

Mount Pl

Renshaw St

Berry St

Hope St

Catharine St

Princes Avenue

Devonshire Rd

Princes Rd

Belvidere Rd

Upper Duke St

Liverpool Cathedral

Upper Parliament St

Upper Parliament St

Central

Duke St

Chinese Arch

Whitechapel

Church St

Hanover St

Paradise St

St George's Hall

Liverpool ONE

Bus Station

Canning Pl

Liver St

The Strand

The Strand

Wapling Dock

Queens Dock

Brunswick Dock

Royal Albert Dock Liverpool

Echo Arena

RIVER MERSEY

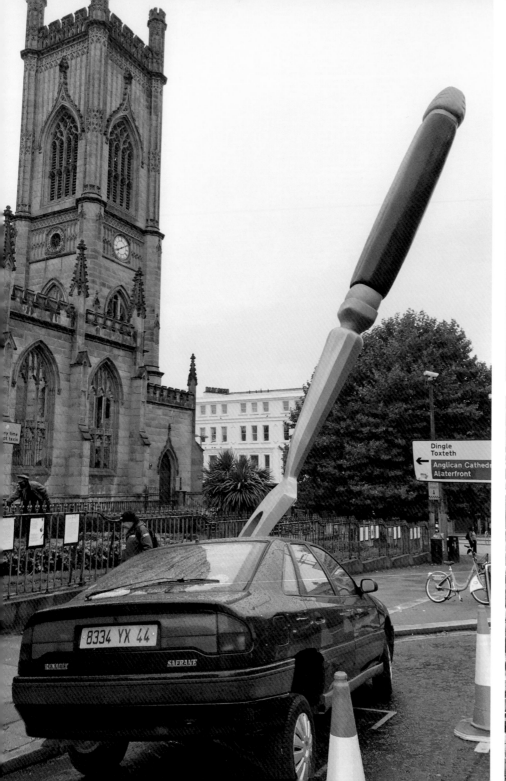

SATURDAY

6 OCTOBER 2018

Three Giants. One City.

With the sun attempting to break through the clouds, the Little Boy Giant and Xolo were well-rested and ready for the day ahead. Breakfast is the most important meal of the day and so they dined on sausage baguettes and fruit to give them vital fuel for the adventures which lay ahead.

A visit to the heart of the city centre, Church Street, was on the cards and the morning heralded a busy day with upbeat crowds lining the route to give the two visitors a warm welcome. As well as discovering teddy bears in wheelie bins, which he gifted to lucky youngsters, cheeky Xolo also managed to win over a local gelato shop, earning himself a delicious-looking ice cream.

The morning's excursions proved a bit much for the canine and a power nap was needed in Williamson Square, lulled to sleep with a beautifully tender song by the Lilliputians.

The Little Boy Giant took in the sights of Church Street, before embarking on a spot of fishing in Derby Square, and what was the catch of the day? A Yellow Submarine of course!

Back together again, Xolo and the Little Boy Giant continued to explore the city streets before heading to Mann Island for a spot of lunch and a siesta.

Elsewhere that morning, after getting a good night's sleep on the ultimate water bed, the Giant arose from his raft and explored the city centre. When he reached Castle Street he encountered a washing line blocking his route – on which, mysteriously, the clothes of the Little Girl Giant were hanging. So what does a Giant do to get around the obstacle? He jumps over it of course!

Following an afternoon siesta, the three Giants continued their travels on a beautifully sunny autumnal day. The playful antics of the Little Boy Giant and Xolo saw The Strand transformed into a race track. Racing goggles donned and steering wheel in hand, our favourite Giant boy meant business, but Xolo gave him a run for his money as they hurtled around the course much to the delight of the audience.

With spectator numbers at an all-time high, all three Giants headed to Clarence Dock for a celebratory evening performance featuring catapulting pianos, giant record players and an excitable Little Boy Giant swinging in the air.

There was a real sense that this Giant chapter was coming to a close and, as crowds headed home, plans were already being made to give the Giants the send-off they deserved.

LIVERPOOL AM

7 **Little Boy Giant & Xolo**
Start 10am (approx)

8 **Giant**
Start 11am (approx)

9 **Little Boy Giant & Xolo**
Siesta 1pm – 3.30pm (approx)

10 **Giant**
Siesta 12.50pm – 3.50pm (approx)

Key

🍴 Food & Drink 👕 Merchandise

🚻 Toilets ℹ Tourist Information

➕ First Aid ⇄ Train Station

👪 Welfare
Meeting Point

Lime St

Central

Lime St

Elliot St

Great Charlotte St

Whitechapel

Crosshall St

Dale St

Tithebarn St

Pall Mall

Moorfields

Victoria St

Lord St

Church St

Hanover St

Paradise St

Castle St

Water St

James St

Chapel St

The Strand

10 Liverpool ONE

The Strand

Salthouse Dock

Salthouse Quay

Gower St

Royal Albert
Dock Liverpool

8

Blundell St

Queens Dock

Wapping Dock

Queen's Wharf

7

Echo
Arena

Kings Parade

RIVER MERSEY

Pier Head

Main Island

9

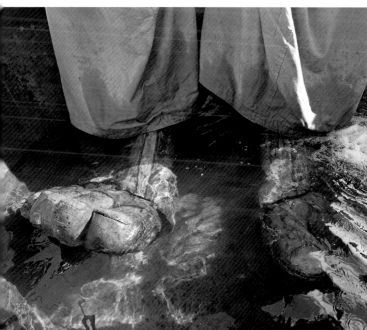

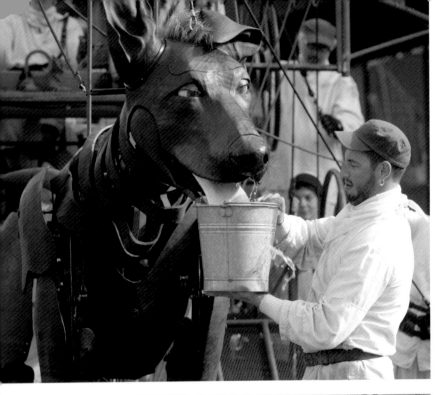

LIVERPOOL PM

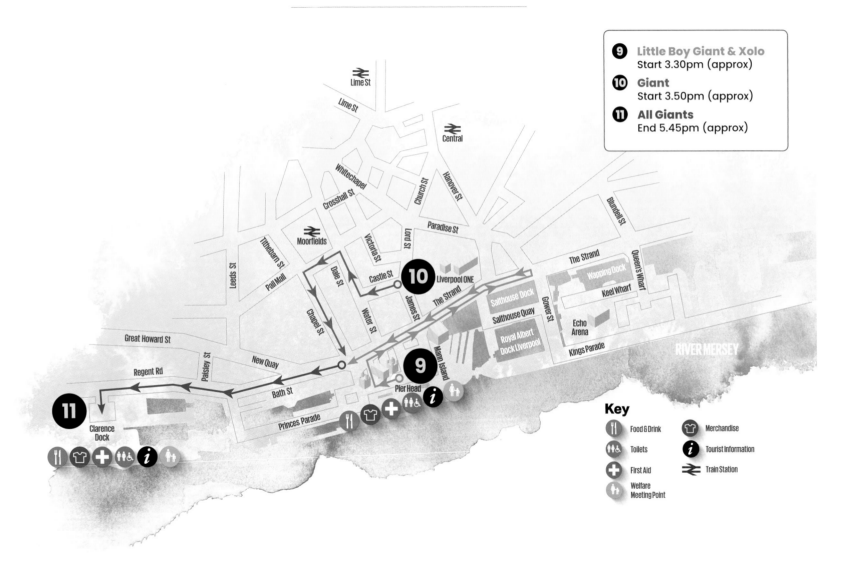

9 **Little Boy Giant & Xolo**
Start 3.30pm (approx)

10 **Giant**
Start 3.50pm (approx)

11 **All Giants**
End 5.45pm (approx)

Key

🍴 Food & Drink

🚻 Toilets

➕ First Aid

👪 Welfare Meeting Point

👕 Merchandise

ℹ️ Tourist Information

🚆 Train Station

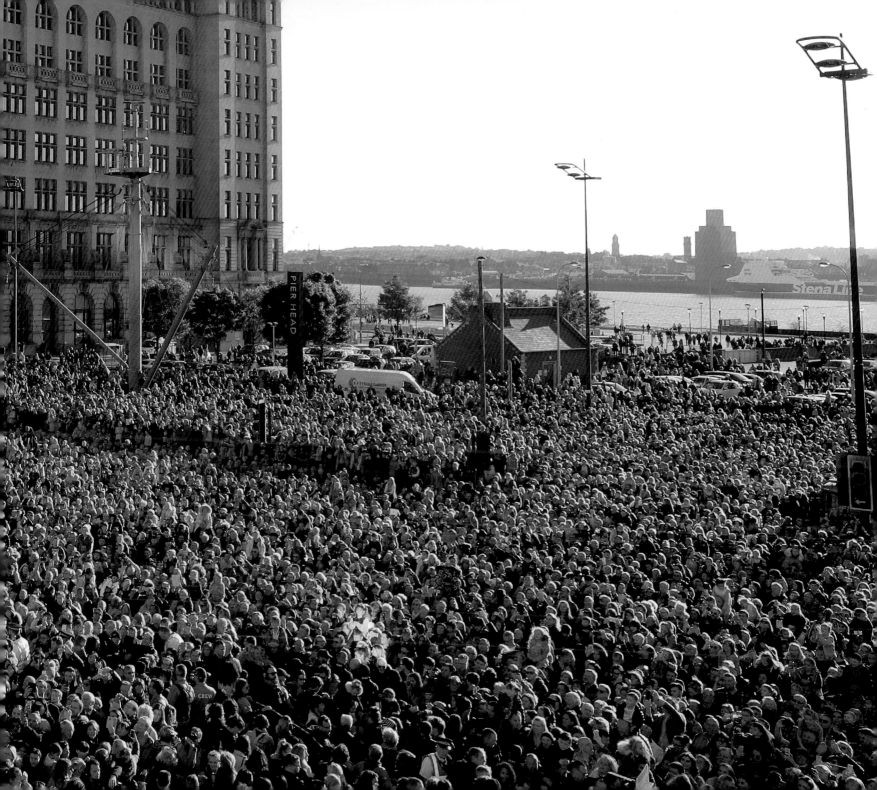

SUNDAY

7 OCTOBER 2018

Time to say bon voyage to our Giant French friends.

The day had arrived. The last ever day people could marvel at the wonder of these Giants. Greeted by a hushed crowd which soon transformed into loud cheers, the three Giants walked together along The Strand in the shadow of the magnificent Three Graces and headed towards Royal Albert Dock Liverpool.

This signalled the end of the Little Boy Giant's journey and his time in Liverpool. The Giant sandal reappeared and became a boat on which the boy lay. Spontaneous rounds of applause broke out as he sailed out on to the River Mersey, with Xolo excitedly running up and down, perching on railings and bridges as he tried to keep sight of his young friend sailing along the dock system home.

With more than 20 miles travelled, the Giant and Xolo had had a tiring few days and were ready for a siesta ahead of their final hours in the city. As they slept on Sefton Street, people flocked to be near them. There was the sense that something was going to happen. The excitement was tangible.

The music gently began, the Giants woke up. And then it happened. The cries of the crowd got louder. The gasps were audible. Some began to cry. She was there. She had returned. The Little Girl Giant had come to say her final goodbye to the city she loves.

A roar went up in celebration. The message spread like wildfire through the hundreds of thousands lining the waterfront. People strained their necks, desperate for a glimpse of this welcome surprise visitor.

Confetti cannons exploded and giant cymbals crashed loudly in celebration as the three Giants paraded towards Royal Albert Dock Liverpool. The riot of sound and colour signified that the event – which had thrilled, shocked and surprised more than a million people – was nearing its climax.

Jean-Luc Courcoult shared a poignant message with the gathered crowds – his love for this city was evident as he shouted, "I embrace you with my Giant arms" before being overcome with emotion.

The Giant sailed away on his raft and the Little Girl Giant and Xolo were driven off into the horizon to another Giant land.

The team of Lilliputians stood to attention along the waterfront, watching the final moments of the show. Tears rolled down their faces as the realisation sank in that the world would never again experience the magic of these Giants.

The show was over. The air of sadness was replaced by the joy of those who had shared this once-in-a-lifetime event.

For the third and final time, people had lined the streets and been transported to a different, Giant world. The story of the Giant, the Little Boy Giant, Xolo and the Little Girl Giant will live long in the memories of all.

It was magical. It was unforgettable. It was inspiring. It was Giant.

LIREPOOL

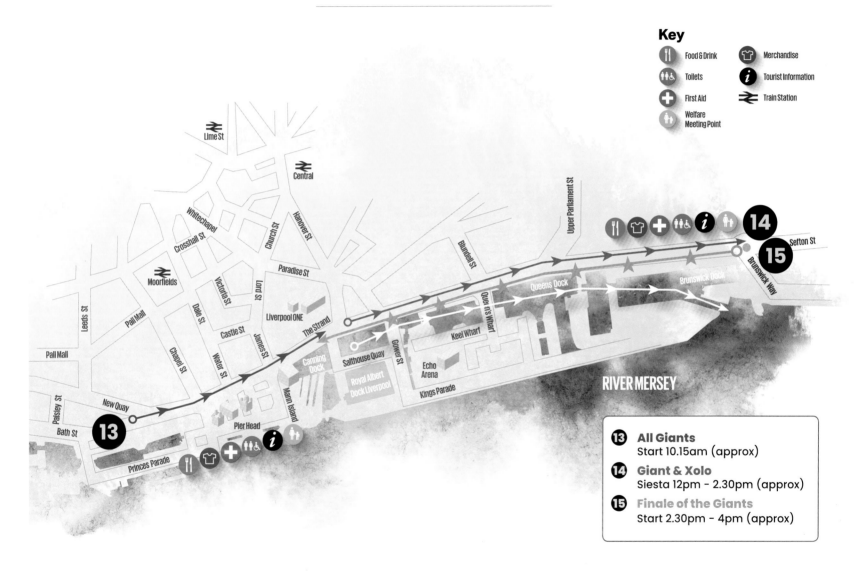

Key

🍴 Food & Drink 👕 Merchandise

🚻 Toilets *i* Tourist Information

➕ First Aid 🚆 Train Station

👪 Welfare Meeting Point

13 **All Giants**
Start 10.15am (approx)

14 **Giant & Xolo**
Siesta 12pm – 2.30pm (approx)

15 **Finale of the Giants**
Start 2.30pm – 4pm (approx)

It was just a story about Giants
who were passing through Liverpool
to transport the dreams of the crowd
above the tides.
As they left the whales followed them.
That's all we've ever been
a whale with a zebra skin
that even the sleeping elephants under the sea
watched pass by.
Liverpool is bleeding and will always bleed in our hearts.
On behalf of this company, Royal de Luxe,
I embrace you with my Giant arms.
Thank you! Thank you! Thank you!

© Written by Jean-Luc Courcoult,
Author and Artistic Director, Founder of Royal de Luxe.

WHAT A FANTASTIC, TRULY SPECTACULAR EXPERIENCE.
Linda Poustie, Penicuik, Scotland

IT TRULY WAS AN INCREDIBLE AND EMOTIONAL EVENT TO WATCH TAKE PLACE IN THE PROUD PLACE I CALL HOME.
Bethanie Davies, Crosby

EVERYTHING THAT IS GOOD IN THE WORLD
Lucia Morgan-Savva, Old Swan

IN A WORLD WHICH IS SOMETIMES DIFFICULT, WHICH RUNS AT SUCH A SPEED, SOMETIMES IT'S NICE TO TAKE A BREATH AND DREAM A LITTLE DREAM.
Jen Higgins, Merseyside

THE LOOK OF ENCHANTMENT ON MY DAUGHTER'S FACE WHEN SHE SAW THE GIANTS JUST SAYS IT ALL! SINGULARLY THE MOST MESMERISING EXPERIENCE OF OUR LIVES.
Rachel Leigh Walker, Cheshire

I HAVE ALREADY SEEN THE GIANTS IN FRANCE, BUT IN LIVERPOOL, THERE HAS ALWAYS BEEN SOMETHING MORE, A PUBLIC ENTHUSIASM, AN EMOTION THAT I FOUND ONLY AT HOME.
Anthony Babonneau, France

NOT ONLY DID XOLO LEAVE HIS PAW PRINT ON MY HEART THAT WILL LAST FOREVER, I ALSO LEFT MY HEART IN LIVERPOOL.

Lerson Tanateeragul, Thailand

THANK YOU LIVERPOOL. THE GIANTS WERE TRULY WONDERFUL.

Pauline Johnson, Liverpool

LIVERPOOL WAS TAKEN OVER BY GIANTS, AND THEY REALLY DO COME TO LIFE. THEY EVEN HAVE THEIR OWN ACCESSORIES AND WARDROBES!

Jennifer Siegrist, Ohio, USA

THIS WAS ONE OF THE BIGGEST EVENTS OF THE YEAR FOR OUR AMAZING CITY. TO HAVE SOMETHING LIKE THIS RIGHT ON YOUR DOORSTEP FOR OUR CHILDREN TO SEE IS JUST PHENOMENAL!

Michelle Jackson, Liverpool

I ENJOYED THE GIANTS AND I WASN'T SCARED. I ENJOYED XOLO BEST. HE MADE ME GIGGLE.

Isaac Forshaw, Nottingham

ONLY A CITY LIKE LIVERPOOL COULD EMBRACE SOMETHING AS AMAZING AS THIS.

Keith Daintry, Liverpool

ACKNOWLEDGEMENTS

A huge thank you to all the people and organisations that made the Giants' visit to Liverpool and Wirral such a resounding success.

Liverpool's Dream was commissioned by Liverpool City Council in a partnership project with Wirral Council. Thank you to all the staff across Liverpool City Council and Wirral Council who worked tirelessly to bring this show to the streets of Liverpool and the Wirral.

We would also like to thank all the members of Royal de Luxe – the artistry and commitment they demonstrated on each visit to the city was truly spectacular.

We would like to extend a giant thank you to Arts Council England, the Liverpool City Region, our partners and funders, who helped to make this event such a success. Thank you to all our volunteers, city stars and benevols who walked every step with us in the footsteps of Giants.

Thank you to all those groups and individuals who made our oversized visitors feel at home, the schoolchildren, clubs and individuals who went that extra mile. Also, a huge thank you to our emergency services across the city, who worked tirelessly alongside us during each visit to ensure the safety of the public. Thank you to the hoteliers, transport partners and businesses across the city who embraced our cultural street theatre with open arms.

Finally, to the people of Liverpool. A heartfelt thank you for all your messages, stories and pictures that you have shared with us over the years. You have taken the Giants into your hearts and helped bring their stories to life.

Special mention to our friends and colleagues Linda Meagor and Etienne Louvieaux, who we lost along the way but who walked with us in the footsteps of Giants.

We hope you've enjoyed the shows as much as we have and that we will see you at our other Culture Liverpool events; please join us on social media or sign up to our newsletter at **cultureliverpool.co.uk**.

For more information on Royal de Luxe, please visit **royal-de-luxe.com**.

(f) **Culture Liverpool**　　(🐦) **@CultureLPool**　　(📷) **Culture_Liverpool**

Liverpool City Council would like to extend a big thank you to all our funders, sponsors, partners and volunteers whose support has helped make this event possible.

    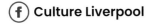    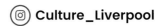